The Many Faces of Masks

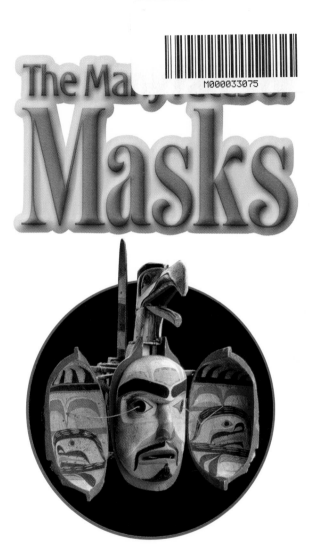

By Cassie Welsh

Celebration Press
Pearson Learning Group

Contents

Introduction

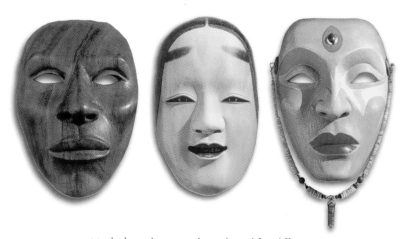

Masks have been made and used for different purposes for thousands of years.

If someone asked you to define *mask*, what would you say? You might say that a mask is a face covering or disguise worn with costumes at celebrations or parties. You might say that it is something that protects the face during work or in battle. Or you might say it is part of a costume that actors wear.

If you answered in any of these ways, you are correct. In fact, masks have been used throughout human history for many different purposes and have played a role in almost every culture.

Mask Faces

Masks are as different as faces and can be made of wood, metal, cloth, leather, clay, or other materials. They can be **anthropomorphic**—having human faces. Or they can be **theriomorphic**—having animal faces.

You could probably make a simple mask with eyes, nose, and lips out of cardboard in a few minutes. More complex masks may be decorated with finely carved patterns, feathers, jewels, or shells. Skilled **artisans** often take months to create such masks.

These two Indonesian men are painting masks to be worn in a Balinese dance.

Way Back When...

Masks have existed for thousands and thousands of years. The first masks were probably animal masks that people wore while praying before the hunt or while hunting. People made these masks between about 40,000 and 10,000 B.C. None of these masks exists today, probably because they were made of animal skins or other materials that do not last.

Several ancient cave paintings have masks in them. **Archaeologists** have found prehistoric drawings of humans wearing animal masks in many areas of the world, including the Sahara Desert in Africa and in North America, Spain, and France.

The cave paintings found at Les Trois Frères, a cave in southern France, are some of the oldest art showing masks in human culture. This cave contains hundreds of paintings of humans, animals, and humans wearing animal heads, which are at least 10,000 years old! The most well-known figure in the cave paintings, the Sorcerer, is a man wearing a stag's head. A stag is a type of deer. Many archaeologists believe that the human figure in this drawing was wearing a stag mask to prepare for hunting.

Stories, Ceremonies, and Festivals

Native Americans of the Northwest Coast carved colorful wooden masks of animal characters such as Wolf, Raven, and Bear. They wore the masks at many festivals, including **potlatches**.

At a potlatch, special events like marriages were announced, and dancers performed special dances wearing animal masks. The dances told traditional stories about the animal characters. These stories, hundreds of years old, were performed and passed down from generation to generation.

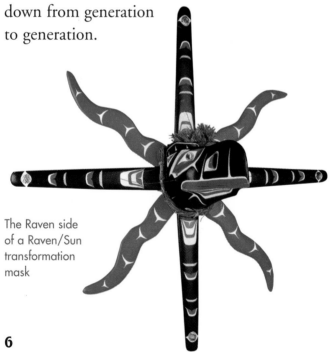

The Raven side of a Raven/Sun transformation mask

The Sun side of a Raven/Sun transformation mask

Many of these dance stories are about Raven, a clever trickster. The mask above tells the story about the time that Raven tried to steal light from the Sun.

The mask is the same mask you saw on page 6. It is a **transformation mask**. The Raven side folds back and reveals the Sun. Its movable parts allowed its wearer to "change" from one character to another to better act out the story. These masks are still important to the Native Americans of the Northwest Coast. They help keep their ancient stories alive.

Across the Pacific Ocean on the island of Bali, Indonesia, masks are still used to perform stories that are thousands of years old. Some of these stories came from India over 2,000 years ago. The Balinese wear highly decorated costumes and special masks as they tell the stories by performing dances.

Masks play a central role in the dances. The dancers' masks and costumes show which characters they are and whether they are heroes or villains. Some masks are so important that only certain dancers are allowed to wear them, and only certain mask makers are allowed to make them, after sacred ceremonies.

Two of the most important masks in Balinese culture are Rangda and the Barong. The Rangda mask is especially detailed—and frightening. Most Rangda masks have long tusks and a very long red and gold tongue. They also have extremely long, tangled hair attached to them. This hair, made of horsehair and other stiff fibers, helps to make Rangda appear especially wicked. Rangda represents evil.

In contrast, the Barong is a creature who represents good. Don't let its pointy teeth and lionish grin fool you! The Barong dance story tells of the Barong's encounter with Rangda. In the dance the two creatures battle each other in a forest.

Mask makers carve much of the Barong mask from wood and then attach decorations to it made of feathers, gold-painted leather, and tiny mirrors. They put a great deal of care into every detail. They must cut small designs into the golden crown. The movable jaw must be just the right size so that the wearer can move it with his own jaw. The mask makers must carefully sew each mirror into the leather. Making a mask like this can take up to four months!

A dancer wearing a Barong mask

The Carnival of Oruro is a pre-Easter festival with brightly costumed masked dancers, music, street dramas, and parades.

In many places in the world, people perform masked story-dances for special festivals. In some cultures these festivals are annual events that attract thousands of people. Often such folk festivals take place in the center of town. Masked dancers parade through the streets, acting out stories and folk tales important to that culture. The Carnival of Oruro, in Bolivia, South America, is one such festival. It begins on the Saturday before Lent, the religious season before Easter.

Dancers usually wear masks made of papier-mâché or plaster of Paris. These materials are molded over wire frames and then painted. The materials absorb the paint easily, so the masks can have even more brilliant colors than a painted wooden mask. Papier-mâché masks are also more lightweight than wood or metal masks, which makes it easier for the dancers to wear them for long periods of time.

During the Carnival of Oruro, the masked dancers tell several different kinds of stories. These stories, though partly made up, still tell a great deal about the history of the Bolivian people.

Many Bolivians today have both Spanish and Inca ancestors. The dance-stories allow them to explore their past from both sides of their heritage.

One dance-story tells of the Inca people and their defeat by the Spanish **conquistadors**. The great Inca Empire stretched across western South America in parts of present-day Bolivia, Ecuador, Chile, Peru, and Argentina before the Spanish arrived in the 1500s.

The Inca dance performed at the Carnival tells of the legendary last Inca ruler, Atahualpa (ah tuh WAHL puh). The Spanish explorer Francisco Pizzaro captured and executed him. The Inca dance celebrates Atahualpa's bravery.

The Inca dance, however, is not the only masked dance performed at the Carnival of Oruyo. The diablada, or devil dance, is one of the most well-known dances in many parts of South America. Some of the most colorful and interesting masks are worn by the diablada dancers. These masks are often decorated with snakes, toads, and other reptiles.

Carnival celebrations began in Europe during the Middle Ages, about A.D. 500–1500, as religious festivals. People in Germany, the United States, Spain, and Mexico today still use masks to celebrate and tell stories during their Carnival festivals.

As in Bolivia, Carnival in Mexico began after the Spanish conquest in the 1500s. When Spanish missionaries arrived in Mexico, they used masked plays and stories to try to change the native people to the Spanish people's beliefs. These masked plays were based on plays that were very popular in Europe at this time.

The missionaries also introduced Mexico to the festival of Carnival. At that time in Europe, Carnival was a popular time of celebration before a period of deep religious thought and fasting. In Mexico, the native peoples adopted much of the new celebration, but they also changed it. They created their own types of masks and added their own stories and dances.

One such Mexican dance, *la danza de los catrines* (lah DAHN zuh day lohs cuh TREE nays)—the dance of the dandies, pokes fun at the wealthy landowners of ages past. The masks worn for this dance are extremely lifelike. Although the mask wearers look through slits in the eyebrows of the mask, they can still blink and wink at people. How can they do this? These masks have glass eyes with false eyelashes. The mask wearer opens and closes the eyes using a string attached to a special spring.

Dancers wearing Catrin masks

You are probably familiar with a Carnival festival celebrated each year in some places in the United States—Mardi Gras. *Mardi gras* means "fat Tuesday" in French. This name indicates that Carnival is, for some people, a day of celebration before a period of fasting. People usually ate a great deal on this Tuesday.

Today the most famous Mardi Gras celebration in the United States takes place in New Orleans, Louisiana. Mardi Gras differs quite a bit from Carnivals in Mexico and Bolivia. During Mardi Gras, people do not usually perform traditional dances. Instead, **krewes**, or private groups of parade participants, organize and pay for parades and parties. They help choose themes for Mardi Gras parades and decorate the elaborate floats accordingly.

They also choose costumes and masks that reflect that theme. Sometimes krewes wear masks that represent historical figures. Other times they wear masks that represent ancient heroes from Greek, Roman, and Egyptian myths. Some people wear simple plain black or white masks to disguise their faces, as they would at a masquerade ball. These different kinds of masks show that Mardi Gras is really a melting pot of many cultures, much like the United States itself.

Honoring Ancestors

Some people, such as the Kuba, who live in the Democratic Republic of the Congo in Africa, made masks to honor ancestors. One of their most important masks, called a **Moshambwooy**, represents their legendary first ancestor and king, Woot. Kuba kings and important chiefs wear it to show honor and respect for Woot.

Moshambwooy masks are decorated with cowrie shells, beads, and leopard fur, which show wealth and status among the Kuba people. The Kuba wear these masks at important ceremonies.

A Kuba man wears an elaborate ceremonial mask.

Another group that honors its ancestors is the Egyptians. The death mask of Tutankhamen is over 3,000 years old and is one of the most famous masks ever made. Archaeologists found it in an Egyptian tomb in 1922, covering the face of the young king.

The Egyptians carefully prepared the dead for an afterlife by mummifying the body and making a death mask, usually from a wax impression of the face. Death masks were often made of gold and gems. The Egyptians placed masks on the faces of the dead to guide the spirit back to the body.

Death mask of Tutankhamen, made of gold inlaid with precious stones

Masks on Stage

Perhaps one of the most popular uses of masks in European and other Western cultures has been by actors in the theater. Masks aren't often used in performances today. But their past importance to the theater is clear in the symbol used for drama—two simple masks, side by side, one frowning and one smiling. The masks stand for tragedy and comedy.

The use of masks in the theater goes back to ancient Greece and Rome. Unlike the gold masks of ancient Egypt, these masks no longer exist. However, we know from paintings that Greek masks exaggerated the features and were probably made of leather or canvas.

The Greek theater masks showed basic expressions such as anger, happiness, or sadness. They also contained a megaphone that amplified the actors' voices, so that everyone in the theater could hear. The large size of the masks and the amplifier were extremely useful in the large outdoor theaters of ancient Greece.

Masks were also used in plays during the Middle Ages and the Renaissance (1300s to 1600s). During the Middle Ages, mystery plays, based on stories from the Bible, were especially popular. There were masked demons, dragons, and the devil. The masks used for these plays were usually made of papier-mâché and were very effective. Some of these masks even thrilled audiences with special effects, such as blowing smoke and fire.

During the Renaissance in Italy, a form of theater called the **commedia dell'arte** (koh MAY dee ah del LAHR tay) became popular. The term means "comedy of art" in Italian. All of these plays were comedies. Actors wore special masks that represented well-known types of characters. The actors wearing these masks "became" these characters and improvised, or made stories up during the performance.

This painting shows masked characters performing in the commedia dell'arte.

One popular character was Harlequin, a comic servant who was very clever. He was an acrobat and wore a catlike mask and colorful patched clothing.

The commedia dell'arte lost popularity in the 1700s. But historians today think that the mime, the clown, and the masquerade mask have all been influenced by the commedia dell'arte theater.

In Japan today, actors perform the still-popular masked **Noh drama**. Noh drama began in the early 1300s and is traditionally performed only by men.

For these dramas there are about 125 types of mask faces—men and women, young and old, and imaginary creatures. The masks are painted in traditional colors to show the character's nature—for example, red for the hero and black for the villain. A white mask is used to show a corrupt ruler.

A mask maker, or **tenka-ichi**, carefully carves each mask. It is made of wood and covered with plaster and a lacquer that gives it a glossy glaze. This light-reflecting glaze helps create the illusion that the mask is changing expressions as the actor moves his head.

A Japanese actor in costume and mask during a Noh drama

The Mask Maker's Process

In some cultures the mask makers are specially trained and are important figures in the community. They are often seen primarily as craftspersons. In some African villages, for example, mask makers are also blacksmiths who make the tools used for mask carving as well. They usually learn the craft of mask making from their fathers or become **apprentices** to skilled mask makers. As an apprentice they learn the secrets of mask making and how to use the tools of the trade.

In some cultures, mask makers must gather materials for their masks. Certain masks can only be made of certain materials. For example, Balinese mask makers make Rangda masks only from the *kepuh-rangdu* or *pule* tree. Mask makers often obtain these special materials themselves or entrust the work to a trusted member of their community.

Once the mask makers have the necessary materials, they begin work. Plaster masks need to be molded, dried, and painted. Metal masks must often be melted and then shaped and decorated. Wooden masks need to be shaped, carved, and painted.

The tools that mask makers use to create their masks are extremely important to them, much as a lucky tennis racket might be to a tennis player. For example, in some African cultures, mask makers carve wooden masks with a special tool called an adz, which has a thin, curved blade. Often a young mask maker inherits this tool from another mask maker. The young mask maker then carries on a tradition by using that same adz.

This African woodcarver is using an adz like the ones mask makers use.

Masks Today

In the past, African mask makers, as well as Native American and Indonesian mask makers, among others, were not considered to be artists. People admired their work more for its representation of traditional characters or people than for its special qualities.

Today some of this attitude has changed. Masks still play a part in traditional dances and stories, but now they are also exhibited in museums and galleries all over the world. Many people respect the mask makers' work for its creativity and originality.

Some mask makers in places such as Bali now make a living selling their masks to tourists and collectors. Many artists, such as Andy Warhol, have created new art based on traditional mask forms. The importance and purposes of masks have developed and changed over the years. Today, masks not only teach us about the world's cultures, they also delight us with their beauty and artistry.

Glossary

archaeologist a scientist who studies the people and culture of ancient times by studying ancient objects, such as drawings or pottery

artisan a skilled craftsperson

apprentice a person who learns a trade by assisting an experienced craftsperson

anthropomorphic having human features

commedia dell'arte a form of comic theater popular during the Renaissance, which featured improvisation and masked characters

conquistadors Spanish conquerors of Mexico and Peru in the 1500s

krewe a private group who organize and pay for the parades and parties during Mardi Gras

Moshambwooy a mask that represents the Kuba people's ancestor Woot

Noh drama a popular Japanese masked drama that began in the 1300s

potlatch a Northwest Coast Native American festival at which a family gave gifts and announced marriages or other special events. The hosts and guests performed masked dances.

tenka-ichi a Japanese Noh mask maker

theriomorphic having animal features

transformation mask a complex Northwest Coast Native American mask, which can change from one animal or character to another (for example, one side might be a sun and the other, a raven)